PICTURES REFRAMED

LEIF OVE ANDSNES | ROBIN RHODE

Владиміру Васильевичу Стасову

Картинки съ выставки

Десять пьесъ для фортепіано

Модеста Мусоргскаго

Цѣна 2 р. 50 коп.

A Monsieur Wladimir Stassoff

„Tableaux d'une exposition"

Série de dix pièces
POUR PIANO
PAR
MODESTE MOUSSORGSKY

Mk. 6.—

Собственность издателя для всѣхъ странъ
В. БЕССЕЛЬ и К°
Поставщики двора Е.И.ВЕЛИЧЕСТВА
С.ПЕТЕРБУРГЪ и МОСКВА.

Propriété des éditeurs pour tous pays
W. BESSEL & Cie
Fournisseurs de la Cour Impériale.
ЗА PETERSBOURG et MOSCOU.

Berlin—Bruxelles—BREITKOPF & HÄRTEL, Leipzig—Londres—New York.
Tous droits de reproduction, de traduction et d'exécution publique réservés en tous pays.
VARSOVIE, chez GEBETHNER et WOLFF.

Imprimerie de musique de W. Bessel et Cie à St. Petersbourg.

PROMENADE 1
KADET (PART 1)

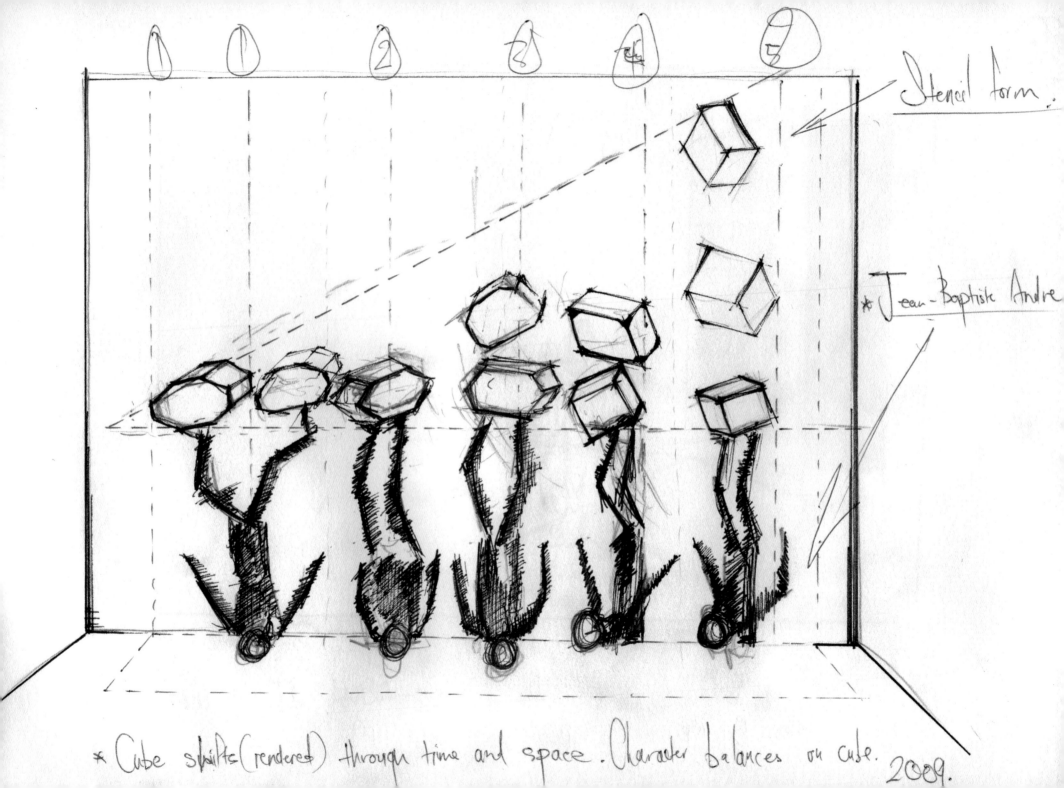

Stencil form.

* Jean-Baptiste Andre

* Cube shifts (rendered) through time and space. Character balances on cube. 2009.

2

GNOMUS
WIRE BALLET

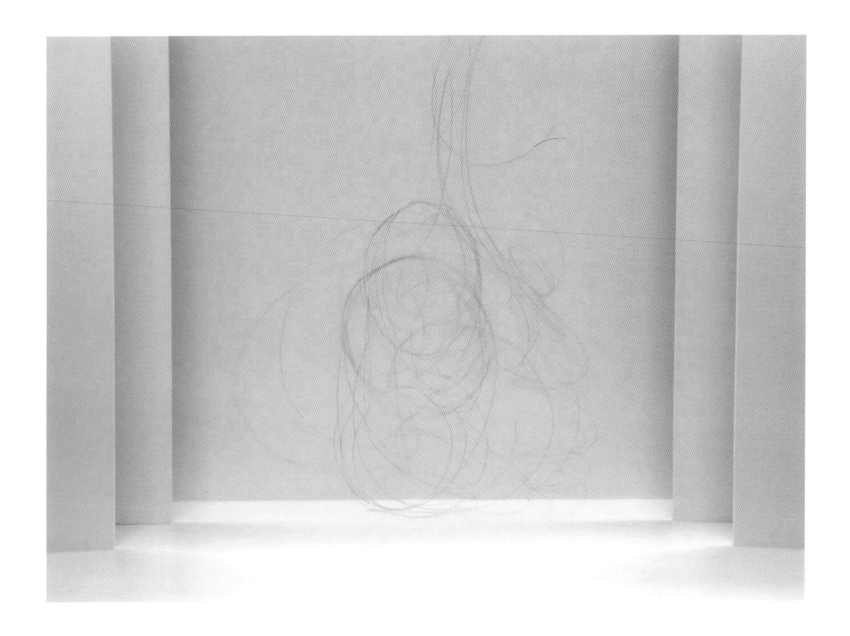

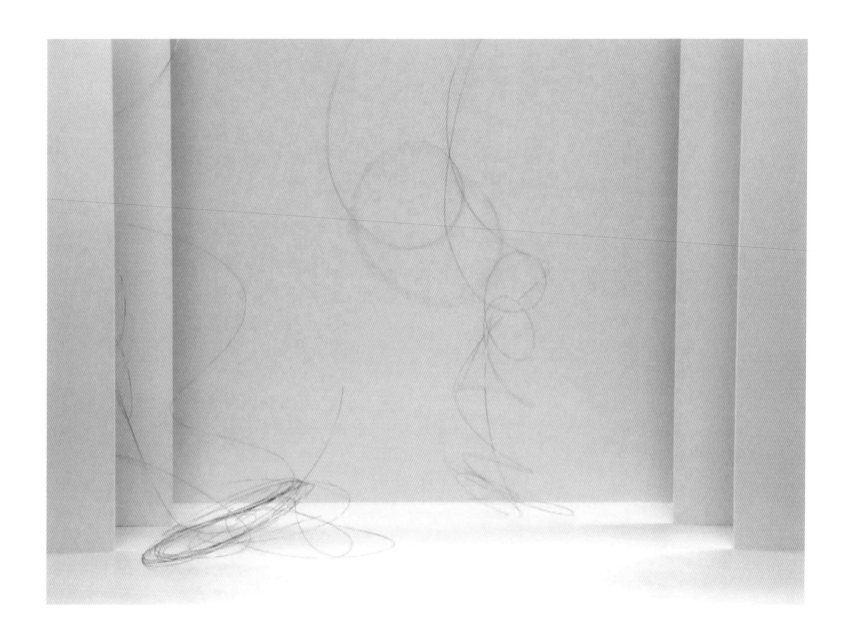

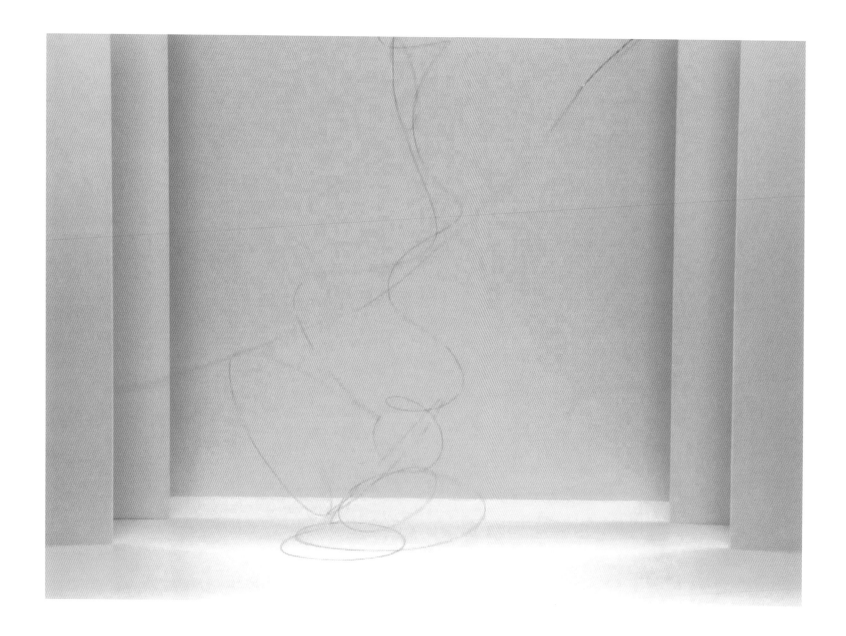

JOINTS

- Stage perspective * Back wall / Side walls / Ground } To be painted white .

- Wire thrown into white stage

+ Camera cuts/ focuses onto movement of wire inside space .

ROBIN 09.

3

PROMENADE 2
KADET (PART 2)

4

IL VECCHIO CASTELLO
MEDIEVAL CASTLE

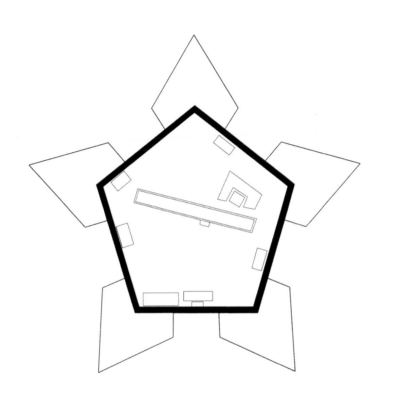
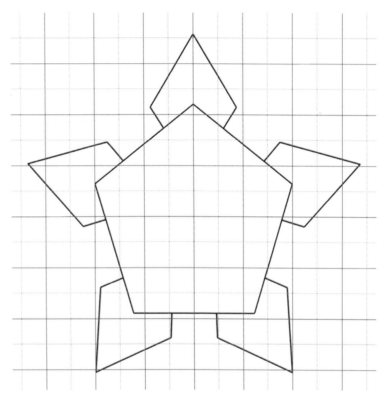

5

PROMENADE 3
PROMENADE

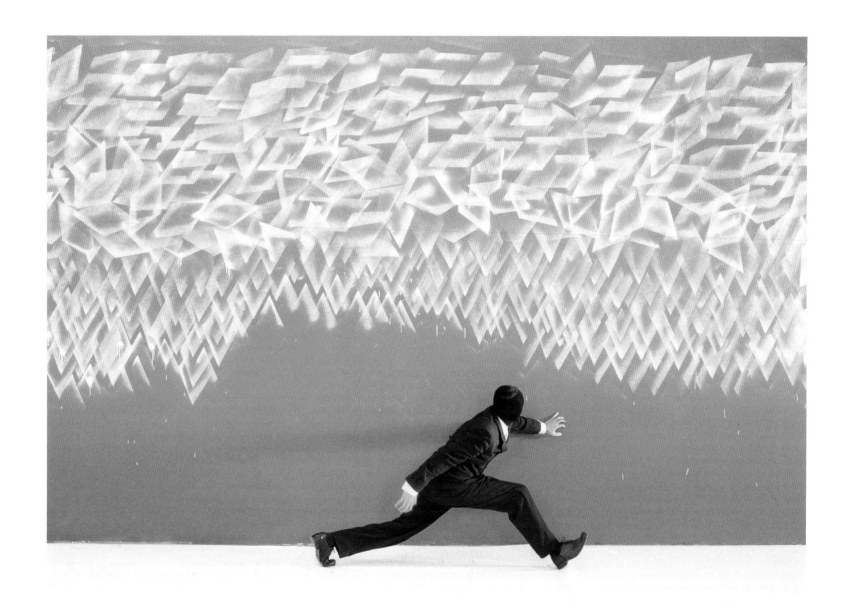

6

TUILERIES
KITE

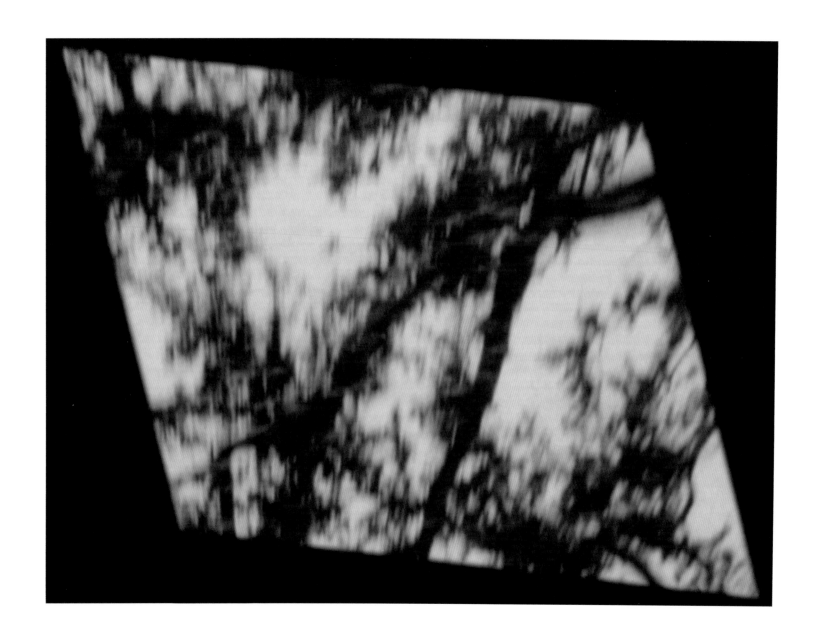

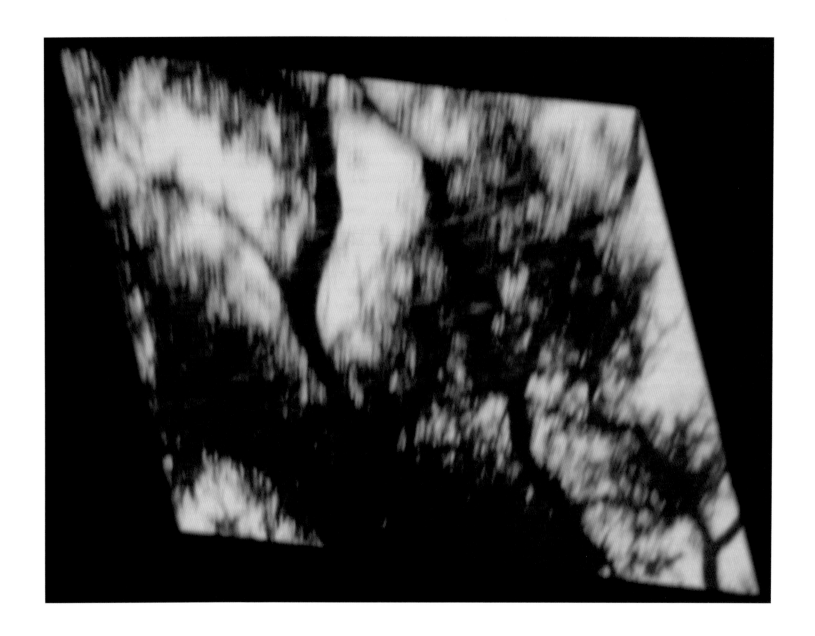

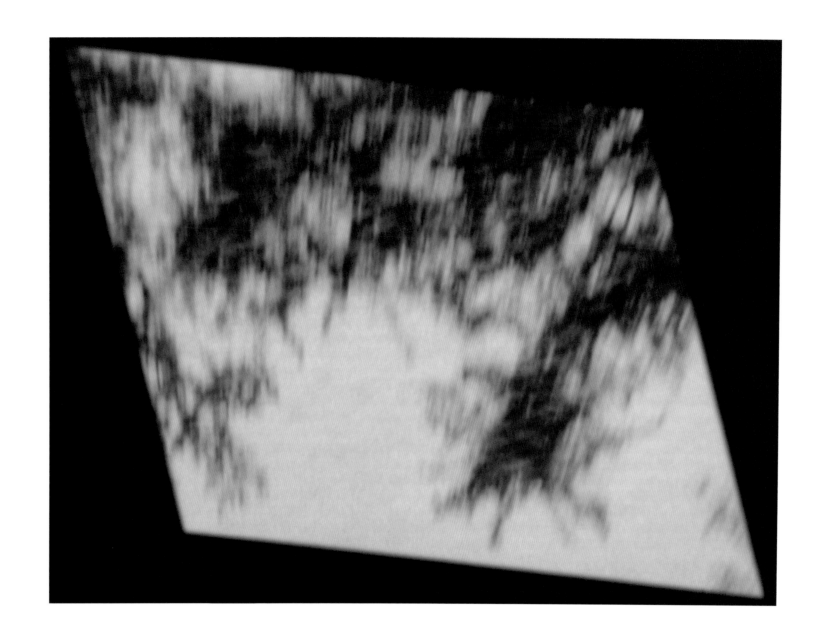

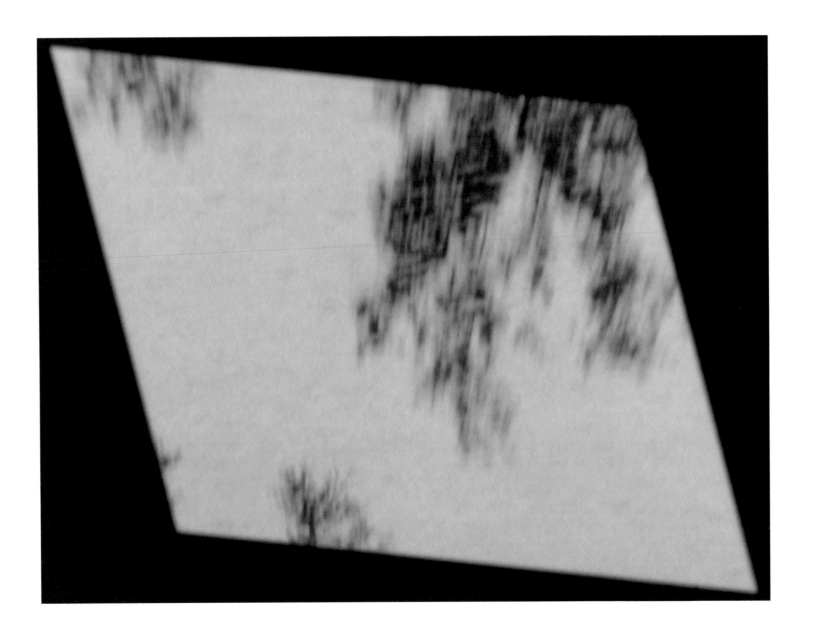

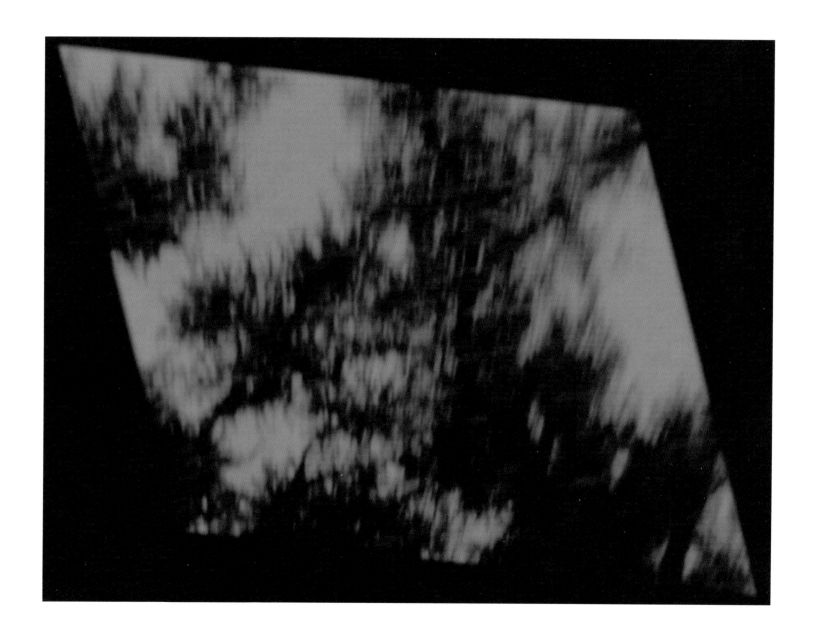

7

BYDŁO
OLD STATION

PROMENADE 4
APPARATUS

9

BALLET OF THE UNHATCHED CHICKS
TRILBI

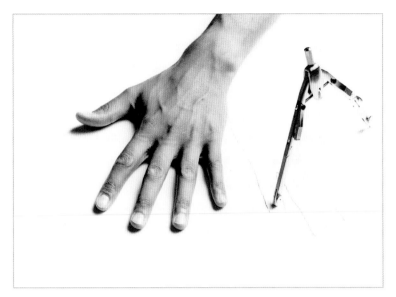

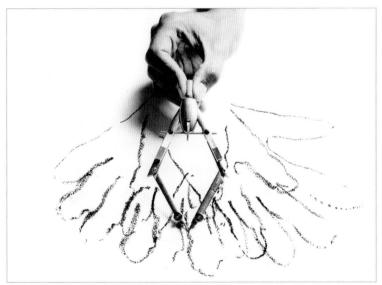

10

GOLDENBERG AND SCHMUŸLE
BANK SYMBOLS

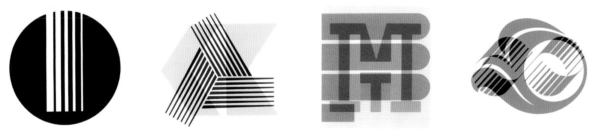

11

PROMENADE 5
KADET (PART 3)

LIMOGES — LE MARCHÉ
CHALK PIANO

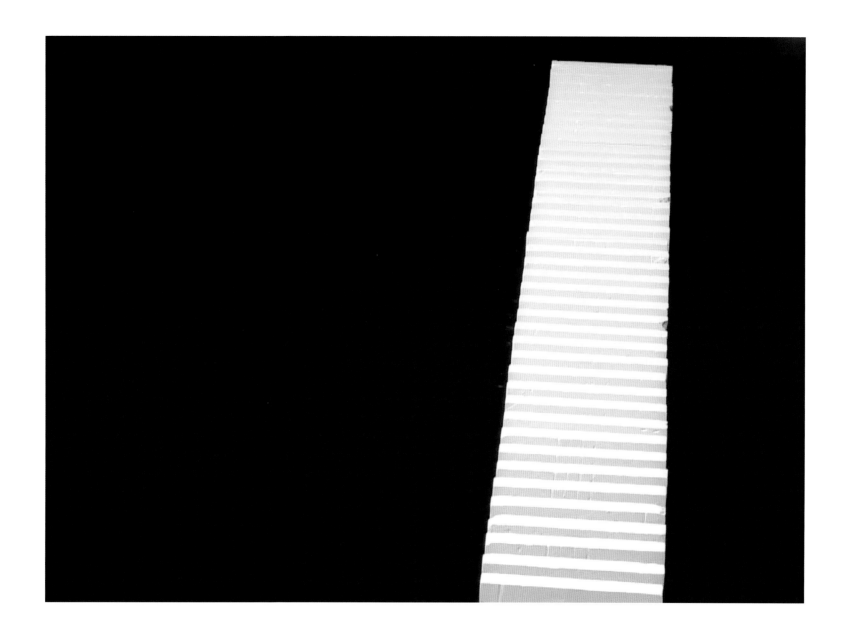

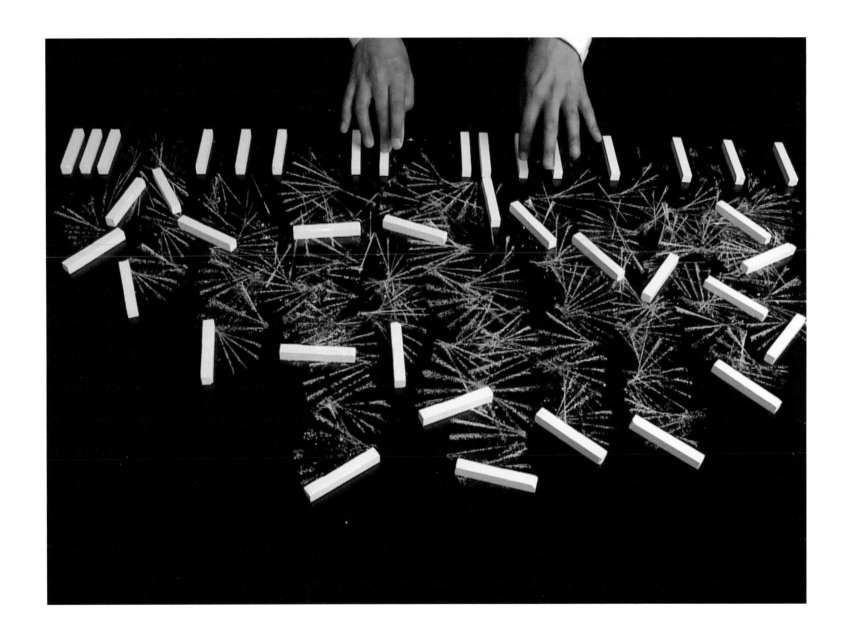

Mussorgsky Piano Project.

- WHITE CHALK (RECTANGULAR FORM)   } White chalk pieces animate itself
- BLACK SURFACE (WOOD 2 X 2 metres). } across the surface creating a drawing.

White Chalk.

Black Surface.

- WORK REFERENCE KEYS 2008.

13

CATACOMBAE — CON MORTUIS IN LINGUA MORTUA
INK STRIKES

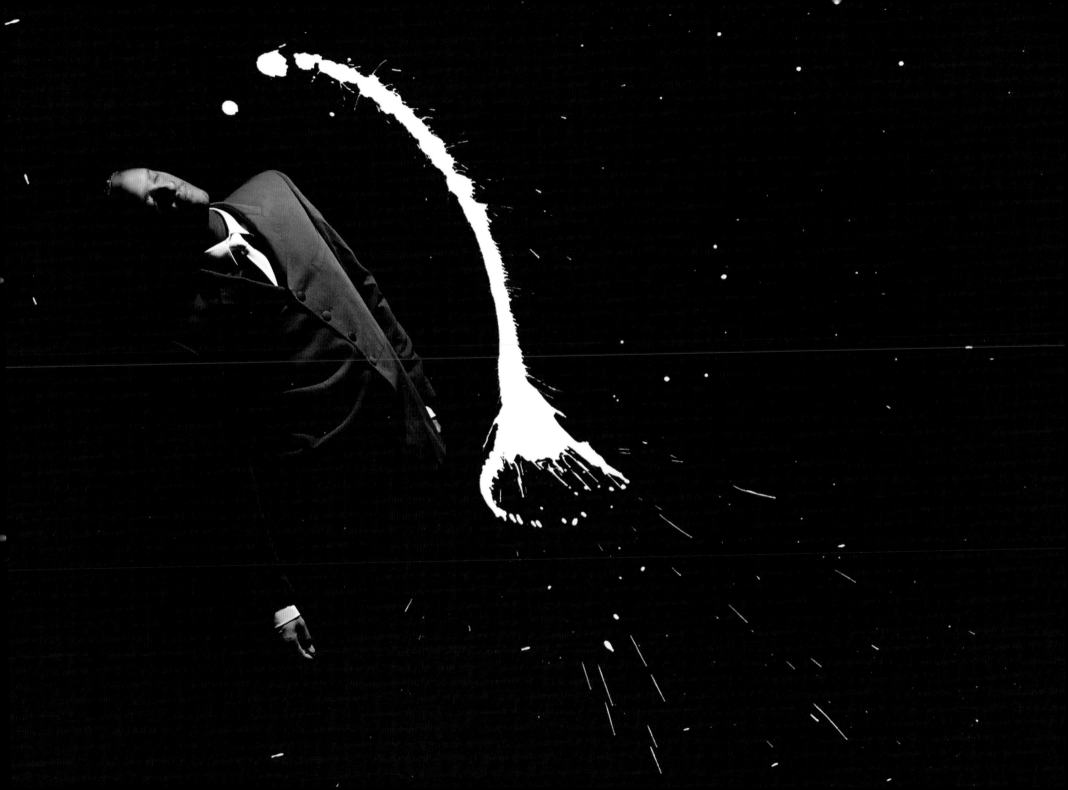

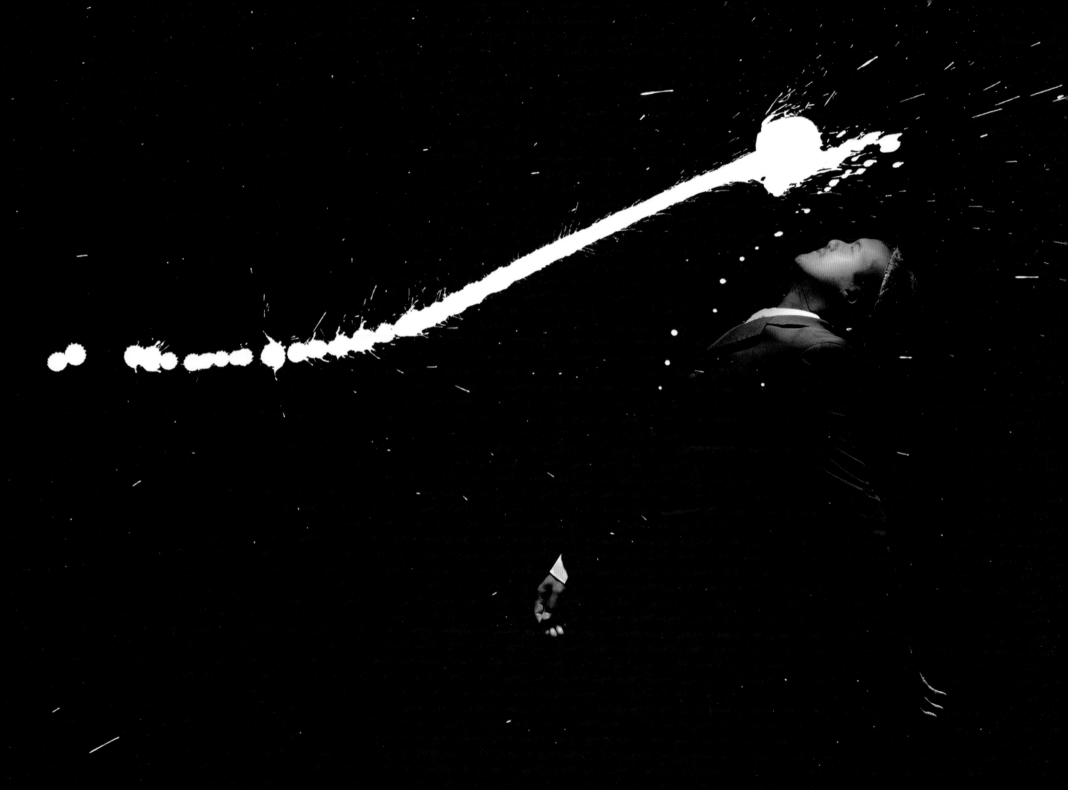

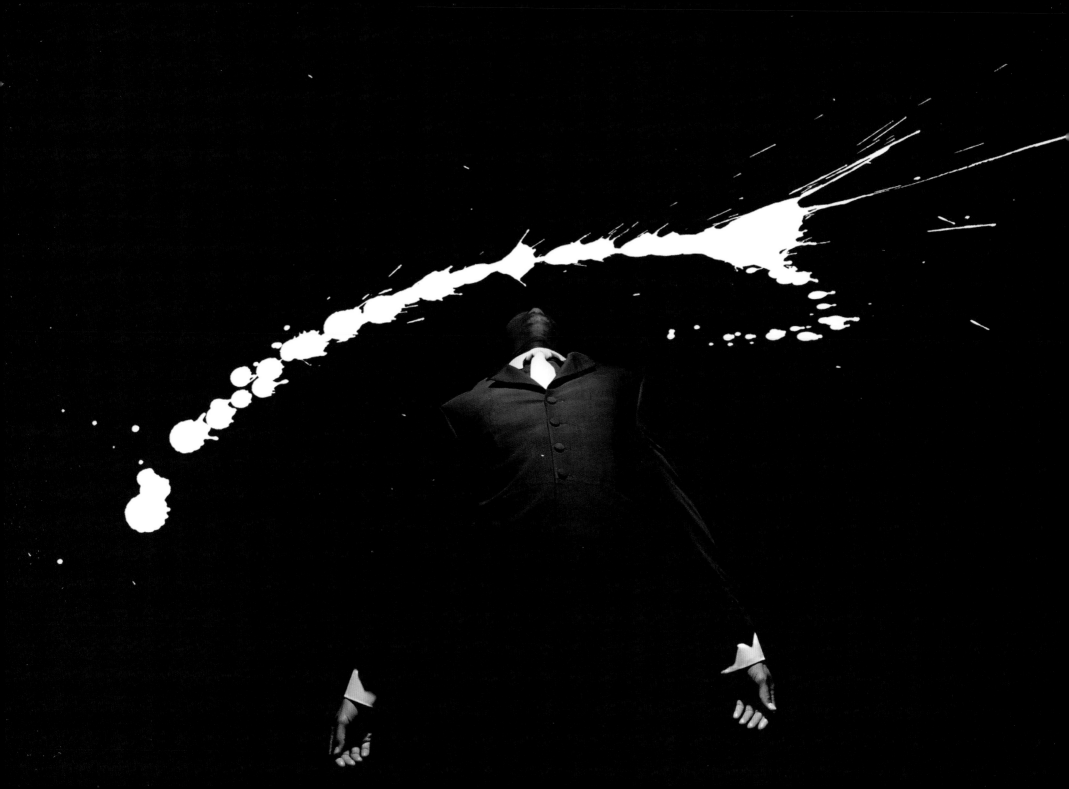

14

THE HUT ON FOWL'S LEGS
BABA-YAGA

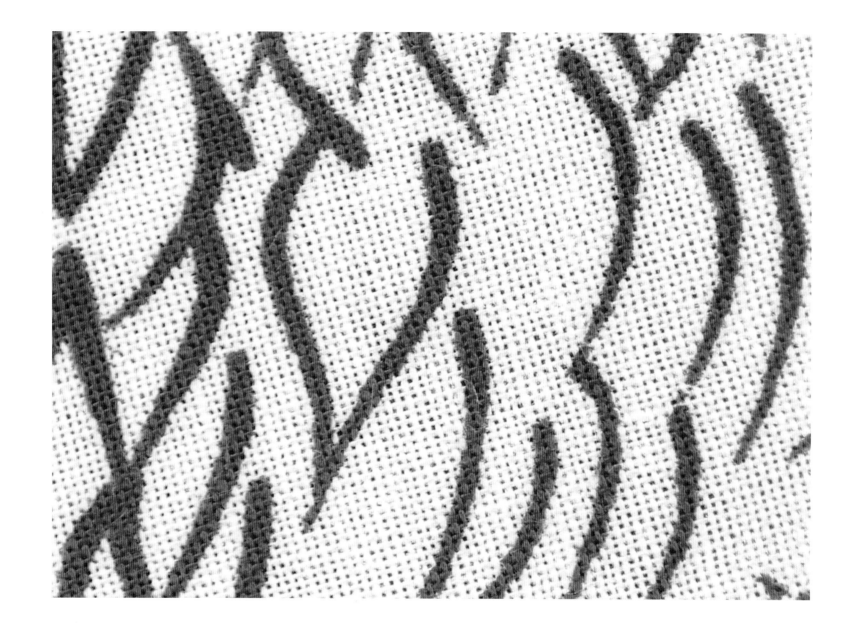

126

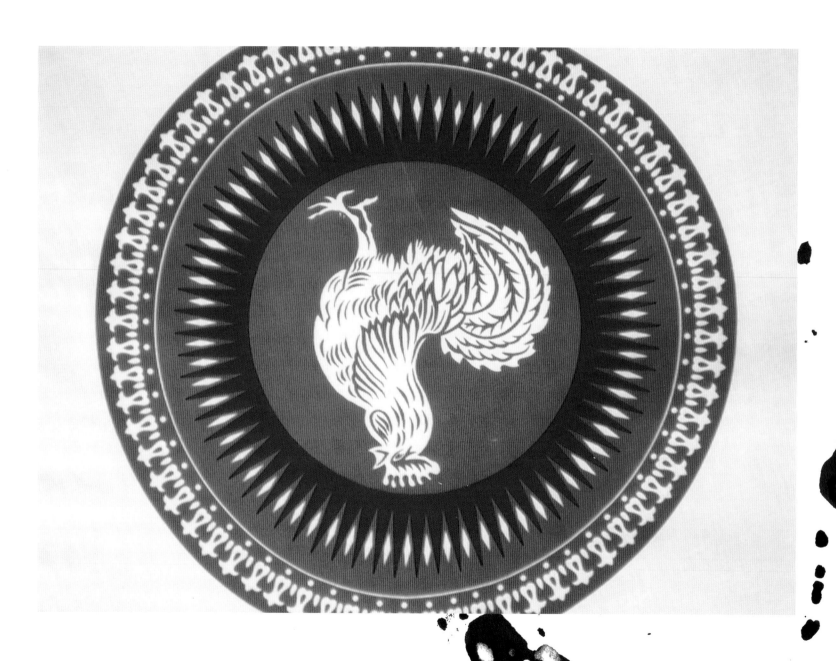

131

15

THE GREAT GATE OF KIEV
DROWNING PIANO

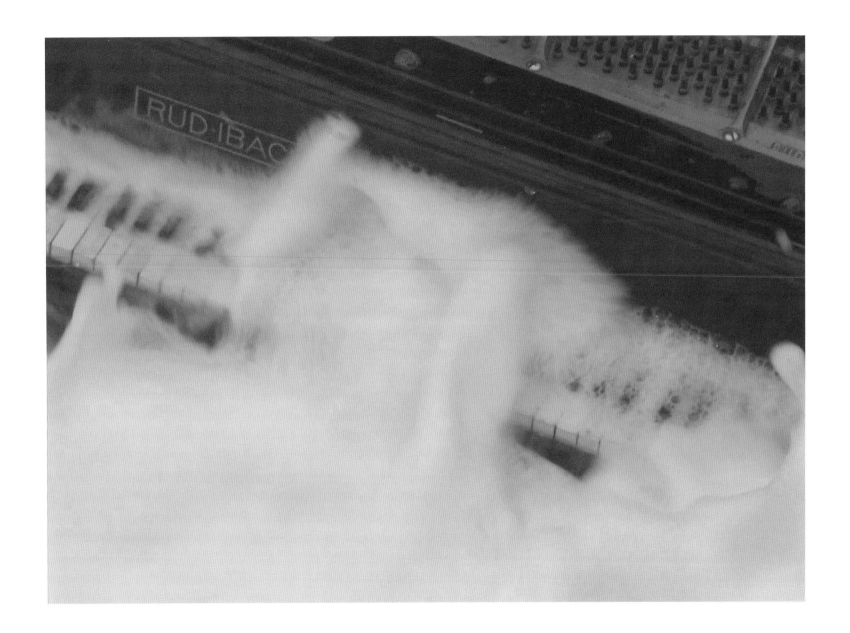

1. PROMENADE 1. **KADET (PART 1)** pp. 3–8
The character in 'Kadet' (Promenades 1, 2 and 5) is loosely based on Mussorgsky as a young man, and refers to his military rank in the Russian army as 'cadet'. The character in the animation represents a youth on a path of self-discovery, his feet grounded on cubes that truncate as they shift through space, engaging in a struggle to define his position in the world. As the cube transcends time, its form begins to change, as if the 'kadet' has placed an exerting force on it. The character remains physically suspended, his feet never touching a given ground, and thus rejecting reality.

2. GNOMUS. **WIRE BALLET** pp. 9–19
On a white theatre stage, tangled piano wires fall from the ceiling to begin an abstract ballet. The wires become reminiscent of anthropomorphic line drawings, three-dimensional drawn studies of the body in space.
   This stage-piece is inspired by Tchaikovsky's *Nutcracker* ballet. The forms within this ballet embody both abstract and anthropomorphic qualities that relate specifically to Gnomus, the original sketch by Hartmann of a gnome waddling on bow legs.

3. PROMENADE 2. **KADET (PART 2)** pp. 21–24
The 'kadet' juggles a truncated cube with his feet, slowly fragmenting the shape. He stands on his hands, feet hovering on the sculptured cube, as we begin to lose sense of up and down, right and wrong. The action is circus-like, playful yet assured, conveying Mussorgsky's stroll through the exhibition.

4. IL VECCHIO CASTELLO. **MEDIEVAL CASTLE** pp. 25–35
This film depicts a forest in the shape of a pentagon. The shape refers to architectural diagrams and models, notably the pentagonal shape of the Castle of Good Hope situated in Cape Town, South Africa. The Cape Castle had been designed and built in the 1660s by the Dutch East India Company in such a way as to repel an attack from any position.
   This visual accompaniment uses the star-shaped forest to evoke the five extremities of the human body – head, two arms and two legs – thus relating to the human figure of the troubadour. The metallic spheres denote man's existence within nature and the tension arising from this given state.

5. PROMENADE 3. **PROMENADE** pp. 37–46
This promenade movement appears vigorous and confident while the recurrent 'kadet' character is assailed by a cloud of diamond shapes, which begins to overwhelm him like a tidal wave. Slowly the geometric forms subside, allowing the 'kadet' to reach out and almost grasp the nature of these abstract shapes.

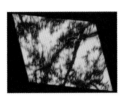

6. TUILERIES. **KITE** pp. 47–56

Hartmann painted a watercolour of the famous Parisian gardens and enriched it by including a group of quarrelling children. The geometric shape of the visual accompaniment appears as a window in the shape of a kite, passing through a path of trees as if guided by a breeze.

7. BYDŁO. **OLD STATION** pp. 57–65

A black-and-white film shows the area surrounding a train station. The metal fence with its barbed wire, the dried grass blowing in the wind, a black bag caught on wire fencing, all depict social decay frozen within a single place. The signifier of the train is a strong political reference to South Africa's past, when many people from rural areas travelled long distances into the cities for employment in the surrounding gold mines. The train and Bydło share a common symbol.

8. PROMENADE 4. **APPARATUS** pp. 67–77

In this Promenade the artist begins to draw a rhombus (diamond shape) on his paper. While engaging with the drawn outline the rhombus appears as a three-dimensional form on the other side of the string grid. The object/subject thus functions as an extension of the artist's imagination: reality appears first as fiction.

9. BALLET OF THE UNHATCHED CHICKS. **TRILBI** pp. 79–89

Hartmann drew a sketch of children in chicken eggshell costumes for the Russian ballet 'Trilbi'. The visual accompaniment to this movement begins with a child formally introducing a caliper/compass into the picture frame, and the frame begins to function as a dance floor or stage. This relationship between child and mathematical instrument has a choreographic spirit. The compass is then let free by the child, and its two legs move across the white surface like a ballerina, leaving arc-like traces.

10. GOLDENBERG AND SCHMUŸLE. **BANK SYMBOLS** pp. 91–95

A black-and-white animation shows symbols taken from banks around the world. As the symbols morph into each other, they become indistinguishable and redundant. The formal property of each symbol functions as an optic device. Its graphic nature symbolises a split-second narrative that becomes frozen on the retina of the eye. These symbols begin to form a representation of our precarious economic climate that is both abstract and relative, inclusive and exclusive.

11. PROMENADE 5. **KADET (PART 3)** pp. 97–100
The 'kadet' reappears, stumbling as if drunk, just managing to balance himself on cubes that become his ground or *promenade* only to vanish abruptly, leaving the 'kadet' perplexed. You might think of Mussorgsky, a notoriously heavy drinker, making his none-too-steady way towards the next picture in the exhibition.

12. LIMOGES – LE MARCHÉ. **CHALK PIANO** pp. 101–112
A break away from Hartmann's pictures explores the idea of the piano as an instrument with which to compose a picture. A row of chalks is lined up to imitate piano keys. As the fingers begin to touch the chalk, the 'keys' appear to shift across the blackened space, creating star-burst lines. The creation of these lines mimics the speed and energy of Mussorgsky's movement, while the pianist struggles to keep up. The chalk keys rotate on the black surface creating a white trace, a remnant of sound evoked by the touch of a finger from the pianist.

13. CATACOMBAE – CON MORTUIS IN LINGUA MORTUA. **INK STRIKES** pp. 113–124
White abstract ink splatters across a black space. They vanish into a void, shortlived, ephemeral, denoting a clear emotive rupture. When the Promenade theme recurs under the title *Con mortuis in lingua mortua*, a character in shadow silhouette is seen standing inside the picture. The character relates to Hartmann, reappearing in a dream among splashes of ink strikes. The white ink and ghost become Hartmann, lantern in hand, shedding light on the depths of the catacombs.

14. THE HUT ON FOWL'S LEGS. **BABA-YAGA** pp. 125–131
The visual accompaniment refers to printed fabrics used by Southern African witch-doctors, known as sangomas, who practice a form of traditional healing that is embedded in their culture. They believe that ancestors in the afterlife guide and protect the living. Such ancestors can give instruction and advice to sangomas in the healing of illness, social disharmony and spiritual difficulties. The colours of white, red, and black refer to a Russian fairytale 'Vasilissa the Beautiful' collected by Alexander Afanasyev. In the fairytale Vasilissa is sent to the house of Baba-Yaga to collect light. There she discovers three riders in white (representing Day), red (the Sun), and black (Night). The story and meaning of Baba-Yaga is addressed in formal, abstract terms, touching on aspects of the spiritual world and its meaning for contemporary society.

15. THE GREAT GATE OF KIEV. **DROWNING PIANO** pp. 133–143
The visual component titled 'Drowning Piano' functions as a powerful motif evoked by Mussorgsky's processional movement. Here we see the piano being submerged in water, slowly drowning as water cascades onto the piano keys, then later inside of the piano. The relentless flow of the water onto the grand piano acts as a metaphor of purging history. Once totally submerged the piano becomes a kind of lost treasure beneath the ocean. The piano as object becomes an antiquity of our time that has been hidden and then discovered before our eyes.

Text © Robin Rhode 2009

CREDITS

Curator: Laurence Dreyfus

PARTNERS

NrK   Lincoln Center   IMG *Artists*   EMI CLASSICS

COMMISSIONING SPONSOR

 Statoil

PICTURES REFRAMED CD

MODEST MUSSORGSKY 1839–1881
PICTURES AT AN EXHIBITION

1		Promenade	1.22
2	1.	Gnomus	2.27
3		Promenade	0.50
4	2.	Il vecchio castello *(The Old Castle)*	4.18
5		Promenade	0.31
6	3.	Tuileries	1.00
		Dispute d'enfants après jeux (Dispute between children at play)	
7	4.	Bydło *(The Ox Cart)*	2.34
8		Promenade	0.38
9	5.	Ballet of the Unhatched Chicks	1.15
10	6.	Samuel Goldenberg and Schmuÿle	2.15
11		Promenade	1.21
12	7.	Limoges – Le Marché *La grande nouvelle*	1.27
		(The Market at Limoges – The Great News)	
13	8.	Catacombae (Sepulcrum romanum)	4.03
		Con mortuis in lingua mortua	
14	9.	The Hut on Fowl's Legs	3.25
15	10.	The Great Gate of Kiev	4.32

		Memories of Childhood	
16	1.	Nurse and I	1.18
17	2.	First punishment (Nurse shuts me in a dark room)	1.27
18		Rêverie	4.37
19		Near the southern shore of the Crimea	2.55

ROBERT SCHUMANN 1810–1856
KINDERSZENEN OP.15

20	1.	Von fremden Ländern und Menschen	1.35
		(Of Foreign Lands and Peoples)	
21	2.	Kuriose Geschichte *(A Curious Story)*	1.06
22	3.	Hasche-Mann *(Blind Man's Bluff)*	0.34
23	4.	Bittendes Kind *(Pleading Child)*	0.57
24	5.	Glückes genug *(Happiness)*	1.14
25	6.	Wichtige Begebenheit *(An Important Event)*	1.01
26	7.	Träumerei *(Dreaming)*	2.50
27	8.	Am Kamin *(At the Fireside)*	0.57
28	9.	Ritter vom Steckenpferd *(Knight of the Hobbyhorse)*	0.39
29	10.	Fast zu ernst *(Almost Too Serious)*	1.51
30	11.	Fürchtenmachen *(Frightening)*	1.44
31	12.	Kind im Einschlummern *(Child Falling Asleep)*	2.25
32	13.	Der Dichter spricht *(The Poet Speaks)*	2.19

61.43

LEIF OVE ANDSNES *piano*

Recorded: 15–16.XII.2008 and 7–9.VI.2009, Henry Wood Hall, London
Producer: John Fraser · Recording engineer: Arne Akselberg
Editor: Simon Kiln · Production manager: Kerry Brown

PICTURES REFRAMED

There are more similarities between Mussorgsky's *Pictures at an Exhibition* and Schumann's *Kinderszenen* (Scenes from Childhood) than might be expected. To me, both cycles are unique in the way they describe concrete acts, situations and emotional reactions. Mussorgsky is theatrical, Schumann far more intimate: he manages ingeniously to make music describe emotions many of us recognise from our own childhood: the satisfying sense of security, the feeling when something becomes almost too serious, the overwhelming drowsiness at bed-time as sleep takes over. But a childlike spirit is present in both compositions. Mussorgsky's story has always made me think of the gallery visitor as an innocent, rather naïve soul (perhaps even a a child) marching in to see the exhibition, in complete ignorance of what he will encounter. In addition to describing the individual pictures, Mussorgsky's music shows us the visitor's unfiltered reaction to the overwhelming world he meets once inside. When he finally encounters himself in the pictures (the gallery visitor's 'Promenade' theme recurs in 'Catacombae', 'Con mortuis in lingua mortua' and in 'The Great Gate of Kiev') the exhibition has become a dramatic, life-changing experience for the innocent human.

Mussorgsky's vision of this composition is significantly greater than his ability to write for the piano. To me, several of the piano version's movements feel almost like sketches, or working drawings. One can easily understand the desire of Maurice Ravel and others to orchestrate *Pictures*; and it is just as easy to sympathise with the pianists who have rearranged the work in order to expand its pianistic timbres. Vladimir Horowitz's ingenious arrangement completely altered my view on the composition. I have taken the liberty of following in his inspiring footsteps, while trying to preserve the melodious Russian-Orthodox expression as well as the fundamental, primitive nature of Mussorgsky's music.

© Leif Ove Andsnes, 2009

PICTURES REFRAMED DVD

PICTURES REFRAMED at the Risør Chamber Music Festival, June 2009

LEIF OVE ANDSNES – REFRAMED (documentary)

Acclaimed Norwegian pianist Leif Ove Andsnes and visionary concept artist Robin Rhode join to re-invent the Romantic masterpiece, Mussorgsky's *Pictures at an Exhibition*. An illuminating and entertaining documentary sheds light on the extraordinary creative journey undertaken by the two artists and a complete performance from the Chamber Music Festival in the beautiful setting of Risør, Norway, is captured on film.

Pictures Reframed at the Risør Chamber Music Festival, June 2009
Director: Torstein Vegheim · Post-production: Håvar Karlsen · Executive producer, NRK: Arild Erikstad
Executive producer, IMG Artists: Kathryn Enticott · Curator: Laurence Dreyfus

Leif Ove Andsnes – Reframed
Produced by NRK (Norwegian Broadcasting Company), Bergen
Recorded June 2008–June 2009 · Created by Steinar Birkeland and Thomas Hellum
Executive producers: Oddbjørn Rossnes and Rune Møklebust · English subtitles: Tone Sutterud

DVD design and development: Johannes Müller, msm-studios GmbH, Munich *msm*
Producer: Johannes Müller · Screen design: Hermann Enkemeier
Audio encoding: Sven Mevissen · Video encoding: Markus Ammer
DVD authoring: Markus Ammer & Jens Saure
Subtitles: Tone Sutterud

THANKS

LEIF OVE ANDSNES

I want to thank personally some really important people who have been instrumental in bringing Pictures Reframed to fruition: firstly, the technical crew and my touring pals: Erwan Huon and Tony Harris. Then all my friends at IMG Artists who have worked tirelessly and with such enthusiasm from the outset: my general manager Kathryn Enticott, Bridget Wrathall, Lena Oliver, Cate Dennes, Elena Kostova, Martha Bonta, Nicole Merritt, Maurice Whitaker, Tristen Hennigs and Dina Hijazi.

My wonderful promotion team: Lucy Maxwell Stewart and Bodil Soderlund at Red House Productions, Albert Imperato and Glenn Petry and the rest of the crowd at 21C Media Group. Thanks also to Stephen Johns, Lorna Aizlewood, Zenovia Edwards, Laura Monks and Elizabeth Chew at EMI Classics for working so hard on our new venture. A big thank you to Laurence Dreyfus, who introduced me to Robin and who has been so supportive in the artistic process. Also to Jane Moss at the Lincoln Center who has shown such a passion for this collaboration all along.

The tour wouldn't have happened without the generous support of StatoilHydro, and a special thank you to Kjetil Undhjem, who believed so strongly in the project from day one.

ROBIN RHODE

I would firstly like to thank Leif Ove for believing in my vision of 'Pictures Reframed'. A warm thank you to my team at Rhodeworks, Nina Mücke, Nathan Menglesis, Bo Christian Larsson and Christoph Müller-Diehl.

Thank you to my friend the dancer Jean-Baptiste André for his creative support. Also to the technical team of Erwan Huon and Tony Harris a.k.a. 'Tony Touch'.

Also thank you to Laurence Dreyfus for her complete engagement and support in this artistic journey. Thank you to Tucci and Lisa at Tucci Russo Studio Per L'Arte Contemporanea as well as Mr Paulo Mussat Sartor a.k.a. 'Mr Mussat'.

Thank you to Perry Rubenstein and Caroline Dowling and the rest of the team at Perry Rubenstein Gallery. Also to IMG Artists, Lincoln Center, as well as Fitz and Co and EMI Classics.

I would lastly like to say a deepest thank you to my family, my partner Sabinah and son Elijah who have both engaged creatively in the project and who have sacrificed so much of their time over the last 12 months in support of 'Pictures Reframed'.

www.picturesreframed.com

Visit **www.picturesreframed.com/deluxe** and sign up for further commentary on the music and imagery of Pictures Reframed from Robin Rhode and Leif Ove Andsnes in English, French, German and Italian.

Enter unique code TRILBI2009 to access this exclusive material